D1216767

The Texas Hill Country

A Child's History

By Stella Gipson Polk

Published in the United States of America
By Eakin Press, P.O. Box 23066, Austin, Texas 78735

ISBN 0-89015-253-5

EAKIN PRESS
Austin, Texas

Dedicated To All Pupils

In The Intermediate Grades.

FOREWORD

I have lived all my life in the Texas Hill Country. It is a land of legend and its hills are filled with history.

In time of drought, it is a harsh land but when it rains its rivers are happy streams and its valleys are covered with wildflowers.

The people of the Hill Country are friendly folk. They help each other in time of need and they enjoy visitors. They keep history alive with their family reunions.

As you read this little book, try to picture the sloping hills, the hot Texas sunshine and the blue northers in the winter.

And the next time you make a snow man will you name him Clarence?

Stella Gipson Polk
Mason, Texas

iii

THE Hill Country . . . a

big land of hills and valleys.

I

The Texas Hill Country is a big land of hills and valleys. It is a land of creeks and rivers. Today it is a land of highways.

But when the pioneers came, there were no highways.

The Fisher-Miller Company promised this land to the pioneers. Some of them had crossed the ocean to live in the Texas Hill Country.

They had landed at Galveston and at Indianola. Later, a Texas hurricane washed Indianola away.

The pioneers bought wagons and oxen when they landed. They bought cows to give milk and chickens to lay eggs. They brought dogs with them to keep the wild creatures from their children.

They thought the Texas Hill Country was a lovely land. The skies were so blue. The clouds were like soft puffs of white cotton. And the only noise in the sky when the pioneers came was when the thunder rolled.

Wild plums were red on their bushes in the hills. Blackberry and dewberry vines grew wild along the creeks and rivers. They had sweet ripe fruit to eat. Persimmons were orange and black and ripe. Sometimes a wild Mustang grape vine covered a postoak tree. The purple grapes hung in clusters. Bees found hollow trees and made honey in them.

It was a wonderful land.

But it was a wild land. The land belonged to the Comanche Indians. There were other tribes but the Comanche tribes were the greatest. It was called *Comanche Land.*

The land had many springs. Sometimes spring water came up from between rocks. Sometimes it came off the hills in waterfalls. Pools of water below the falls made fine swimming holes. Also they made fine pools for washing clothes.

The mothers rubbed soap on the dirty clothes and laid them on flat rocks by the pools. They then beat out the dirt with a heavy stick. They called the stick a battling stick.

There were no houses in the Hill Country when the pioneers came. But the Texas Hill Country has many oak trees. Some are postoak and blackjack oak. Some are liveoak. Also there are Spanish oak and shin oak. Oak is good for building homes.

The pioneers built near springs so they could have water for their cabins. They cut off the limbs and made tree trunks into logs. They built their cabins with two rooms. There was an open space between the two rooms. It was called a dog run. The dogs slept there at night. Some cabins had a tiny room upstairs called a cupola. The cupola had windows so the fathers could watch for the Indians. All cabins had holes in the walls to put a

THE CLOUDS are like soft

puffs of white cotton.

gun through if the Indians came. They called the holes gun ports.

Each cabin had a big fireplace. Some cabins had two fireplaces. The fireplaces were built of stones the pioneers found on the land. All fireplaces had wide chimney throats. Pioneers said when there was no smoke coming from the chimney they could look up at the stars through the chimney throat. They could even see their cows coming off the hills to be milked when the day was done.

Each family helped other families build their cabins. The men laid the logs for the walls. The women cooked over open fires. Some of the men hunted the white-tailed deer or the wild turkey for meat. Sometimes they killed the buffalo.

The children ran and played hide-and-seek. The mothers were afraid for them to run in the hills. Grandpa had said there were snakes in the Hill Country. The Hill Country has four poisonous snakes. They are:

The rattlesnake

The copperhead

The Coral

and the

cotton-mouthed moccasin.

The rattlesnake coils before it strikes but it can coil quick as you can wink your eye. Some rattlesnakes have diamond patterns on their backs. They take a bit of the color of the land they live on. They have two fangs that carry poison. When a rattlesnake is angry it has a bad smell.

The copperhead is the color of copper but it takes on the color of the land it lives on. It has two little fangs like needles. The copperhead strikes

BIG rattlesnakes are still around the Hill Country today.

fast. The little fangs sink deep into the skin and they carry a poison.

The coral snake is rare in the Hill Country. Its fangs carry poison. It is bright in color. There are bands of red and yellow and black on its body. The red and yellow bands are side by side. Grandpa had the children say:

"Red on yellow
Kill a fellow."

Then Grandpa told the children about another little snake in the Hill Country that has bands of red and black and yellow around its body. But it is not poisonous. The black band is always between the red and yellow bands. He had the children say:

"Red on black
Poison lack."

Grandpa took his pipe out of his mouth. "Children, listen to me. The cotton mouth moccasin is not only poisonous it will chase you. There are many moccasins in the lower Hill Country but only the blunt-tailed cottonmouth is poisonous. Sometimes when it is angry it will get into a man's boat while he is fishing."

As soon as the pioneers had a cabin built they had a dance. Uncle Eb tuned up his fiddle. Old Mose took his guitar off the wall and young Henry found his mouth organ in the pocket of his Sunday pants. He called it a French harp. They played *Cotton-Eyed Joe, Buffalo Gal, Old Joe Clark, Jimmy Crack Corn* and *Skip To Me Lou, My Darling*.

They made the hills sing with their happy music.

Everybody danced until the moon went

down. Then they went home.

Some nights when Grandpa leaned his chair against the wall outside the cabin, the children begged, "Tell us about the Indians, Grandpa."

Grandpa shook the ashes from his pipe. Then he would begin:

"Once upon a time, Mother Reeves was left alone in the Hill Country with her two babies. Father Reeves had to go in the ox wagon to Fredericksburg to buy flour and meal at the grist mill. A grist mill is where pioneers ground their grain.

"The babies were playing on the floor. Mother Reeves heard an owl hoot. She did not want the owl to eat her chickens. She got the big gun from over the door and went outside.

"She heard the owl hoot again. This time it did not sound like an owl.

"Indians!"

She ran back inside the cabin and bolted the door.

"The Indians ran yelling to the door. They beat on the door with their tomahawks. Mother Reeves looked at her babies playing on the floor. What was she to do? She had a big pot of water boiling in the fireplace. She took the pot of hot water off the hook and ran upstairs to the cupola. There was a window in the cupola above the Indians. She leaned far out the window and threw the boiling water on the Indians. Now the Indians really had something to yell about. They ran. Mother Reeves thanked God and went down to her babies."

Grandpa told the children about the birds. He said in the spring the whip-poor-will bird always waits until Grandma lights a candle in the evening. Then it moves close to the cabin to sing everybody to sleep.

He told how the little wren likes people and builds its nest near the cabin. And if Grandma hung Grandpa's shirt on the clothes line the little wren would build its nest in the shirt pocket.

The bird Grandpa liked best was the Hill Country quail. The pioneers called the quail Bobwhite. Grandpa liked to watch them walking in coveys. All of them talked at the same time. Once he had seen a little papa quail strut. He said it beat a turkey gobbler.

He had the children say:
   "Bobwhite, Bobwhite,
      Are your peas all ripe?
         No, Bobwhite,
            Not quite
               Not quite."

Grandpa did not like the screech owl very much. He said the screech owl is not a happy bird like the mockingbird. A mockingbird gets so happy when it sings it dances up and down on the tree limbs.

Grandma always turned the pocket of her apron wrong side out when the screech owl cries. She said that made the screech owl hush.

Grandpa told how the blue jay sings to tell you about fun and good times. And when a redbird sings it means you will get some money.

The moon rose over the trees. The children could see a man's face in the moon.

Far off in the hills a turtle dove called its sad cry. Grandpa said it cried to tell the sick and lonely they were loved.

"Grandpa, how do you know all these secrets?" the children asked.

Grandpa knew
These secrets
But he
Never told.
The hills also
Know these
secrets but
they never
tell.

Words to Remember

children	pioneers	noise
study	Fisher-Miller	persimmon
Texas	company	creatures
country	promised	fruit
valleys	Galveston	purple
highways	Indianola	Mustang
clusters	postoak	apron
hollow	blackjack	pocket
Comanche	Spanish	Fredericksburg
tribes	cupola	unbolted
battling	chimney	quail
pattern	throat	secrets

AUTUMN comes to

the hill country.

II

Autumn came to the Texas Hill Country. The pioneers called autumn fall. Oak leaves were yellow now and orange and brown. Sumac bushes turned so red the children thought the hills must be on fire.

Pecan trees shed their leaves along the creeks and rivers. Their brown nuts fell on the leaves. The children gathered the nuts. "Mama," they cried, "the hills have such pretty colors. Somebody must have painted them."

The mothers smiled and filled their baskets with nuts. The nuts would be good in cakes. They would be good to eat on winter nights around the fire.

The children showed Grandpa a vine climbing a postoak. "Such a pretty vine, Grandpa. Its leaves are turning red."

Grandpa took his pipe out of his mouth. He shook his head. "Poison ivy," he said. "Do not touch." He showed the children the three points like three fingers on each leaf. He had them say:
"Fingers three
Quickly Flee."

Along the creek banks a pretty vine climbed over a granite rock. "This is a good vine," Grandpa told them. "It is called a Texas Virginia creeper. See its leaves. Each leaf has five points like five fingers." He had the children say:

"Fingers five
Stay alive."

A vine covered an agarita bush. It had silky white down that blew with the winds. "Old man's beard," Grandpa told them. "Like my beard."

The children laughed. "Grandpa, the silky white down does look like your beard."

That night a moon like a big orange wagon wheel rose above the trees. The pioneers called it harvest moon.

The nights grew cool. Grandma and Grandpa and Mama and Papa sat with the children around a big fire in the fireplace. Grandma and Mama were piecing a quilt top. They cut scraps of cloth into pretty shapes and sewed them together to make a quilt top that looked like a flower garden. The name of the quilt was "Flower Garden."

"Grandpa," the children begged, "tell us a story about some good Indians. You said some of the Indians in the Texas Hill County are good Indians."

Grandpa put a big chunk of blackjack oak on the fire. It made a bright orange flame. Papa dozed in his chair. He had cut wood all day. He was tired. Mama and Grandma sewed more pretty quilt pieces. Grandpa took a little twig from the fire and lit his pipe. Then he began:

"There was this preacher at Fredericksburg settlement. He was a circuit rider preacher. A circuit rider preacher rides to many settlements to tell the pioneers about God.

"Preacher Grote left Fredericksburg to preach at Castell. Castell is a little settlement across the Llano River. But when Preacher Grote rode into the Llano he saw a big rise coming down. He rode his horse to a little island in the river. He was tired. He took off his saddle. He lay down with his saddle for a pillow. Soon he was asleep.

"Some Comanche Indians saw Preacher Grote asleep on the island. They swam to the island to help him across the river. But Preacher Grote could not swim. The Indians took the rope from the saddle. They tied one end of the rope to a tree on the island. They swam to the river bank. They tied the other end of the rope to a tree on the bank. Then they swam back to Preacher Grote.

"One Indian led the horse beside the rope. Preacher Grote held to the horse's tail. An Indian swam on either side of Preacher Grote.

They came to Castell.

The pioneers gave Preacher Grote dry clothes. They gave him hot food. Under a big liveoak tree in the yard Preacher Grote told them about God. They sang songs. Then the people knelt with Preacher Grote under the big oak tree and gave thanks to God."

That night as the children lay on their trundle beds they heard wild geese honking above the cabin. They went outside. In the moonlight they could see the geese. The geese flew in the shape of a big V. The point of the V was south. The children thought the cries of the geese were sad.

Grandpa came outside. He told the children,

FISHING is fun in

a Hill Country pond.

"When you hear the geese coming back in the spring their cries will be glad, for winter will be over."

That day while they ate their noon meal of wild turkey and corn pone and turnip greens and milk, Grandma and Mama told Grandpa and Papa they wanted a well. They did not like to carry all their water from the spring.

Grandpa and Papa shook their heads. "Digging a well is hard work," they said.

But Grandma and Mama wanted a well.

Grandpa went down to the creek. He cut a little limb from an elm tree. The little limb was shaped like a wishbone. It still had sap. Grandpa had to have a limb with sap. Sap is the juice in a tree or a plant. Grandpa had to get the limb before the sap went down in the winter.

He held the stick with his two hands. The point was to the sky. Then Grandpa walked with it around the cabin. This was the way pioneers hunted for water under the ground. They called it "water witching."

The point of the stick still turned to the sky.

Grandpa walked to some liveoak trees back of the cabin. The point of the stick turned down—and down—and down. It began to dance. Grandpa said to Mama and Papa, "Here is where we can get plenty of water. Right at the kitchen door." Grandpa put the little stick on the kitchen shelf. His water witching was done.

In the night the children heard a big noise. It came closer—and closer—and closer. They ran to the cabin door. Grandpa and Papa were in front of the cabin with their big guns. Grandma and Mama were making breakfast. They looked worried.

"Grandpa, what is it?"

"Stay in the cabin, Children. A big herd of buffalo is coming over the hills. There are thousands of them. They must not get to the cabin. I am afraid we have built our cabin on a buffalo trail. They may have been using this trail for a hundred years."

On came the big, shaggy buffaloes. The children peeked through the door. The buffaloes made such a dust the children could not see the sky.

They came by the cabin all day long. The children could not go outside. Grandpa and Papa could not go outside. When the buffaloes came too near the cabin, Grandpa and Papa fired their big guns.

"Grandpa, where are the buffaloes going?"

"They are going south like the geese. Maybe they have eaten all the grass where they came from. Maybe they hunt for more grass where the south winds grow warm. This is their trail.

"Maybe they want to tell us this is their trail. Maybe they want to tell us we have built our cabin in their trail.

"But, Grandpa, we could not know."

"No, children, we did not know. The white-tailed deer say the Hill County is their land. The wild Longhorn cows say the Hill Country is their land. The Comanche Indians say it is their land. Maybe if we try hard this Hill Country can be land for all of us."

That night as they sat by the fire they heard a scream like a woman in great pain. The children ran to Grandpa and Papa. They were afraid.

"That is a panther," Grandpa told them. "The Texas Hill Country has many panthers.

"Tell us a panther story," the children said, "so we will forget to be afraid."

"Not tonight, Children. Time for bed. Tomorrow night I will tell you about Henry's mother and the panther."

"Who is Henry, Grandpa?"

"Grandpa, how do you know all these secrets?"

Grandpa knew
    these secrets
        but he
            never told.
The hills also
    know these
        secrets but
            they never
                tell.

Words to Remember

autumn	points	quilt
sumac	granite	chunk
gathered	agarita	settlement
painted	beard	Llano
filled	laughed	island
ivy	piecing	Grot-ee

tied	honking	trail
knelt	witching	scream
clothes	worried	pain
pone	thousands	afraid
juice	buffaloes	panthers
elm	Longhorns	Castell

HORSEBACK riding with papa.

18

III

The nights grew cold. Mama and Grandma put heavy quilts on the beds. They called the heavy quilts comforters. Some of these heavy quilts were filled with goose feathers. They were very warm.

"Now, Grandpa," the children begged, "you promised to tell us a panther story."

Papa threw a big chunk of wood on the fire. The fire made the room bright with light.

Grandpa puffed on his pipe. He made a few smoke rings, then he began:

"Henry's mother lived near the little settlement of Castell and on the banks of the Llano River. One day she wanted to ride a few miles down the river to visit with another mother.

"Henry saddled his mother's mare. The mare's name was Daisy. Daisy had a pretty little brown colt named Dandy. Henry was afraid the Indians might capture his mother. Not all Indians are good like the Indians who helped Pastor Grote across the Llano River. "Mother," Henry said, "Maybe I ought to saddle Nellie and ride with you."

"Nonsense," Henry's mother said, "I am not afraid of Indians. I can shoot as well as any

SHEEP on a farm

in the Hill Country.

man." She got into the saddle. Henry handed up his baby brother. The baby was three months old. Then Henry handed his mother her gun. His mother kissed Henry good-bye then Daisy trotted down the banks of the river. Dandy ran and capered about on his long legs. Dandy was a happy little brown colt.

"The river made a big noise as it tumbled over the rocks. Such a lovely day. Birds sang in the trees and little wildflowers lifted their faces to the sunshine.

"Then Daisy began to rear and scream. Dandy ran and got close to his mother. Dandy was scared. Henry's mother wondered what had scared the mare and her colt. She looked at the trees on either side of the river banks. There were no Indians. She looked behind her and her heart almost stopped beating. Behind her was a big panther just ready to spring on Dandy's back. Panthers like the taste of horse meat. They like young colts for colts have tender meat.

"Henry's mother looked down at the baby. He was sound asleep in the crook of her arm. She looked down at the gun she held in her right hand. 'Oh, God,' she prayed, 'help me.' Then she turned Daisy around fast and shot the panther between the eyes.

"Henry skinned the panther. Its hide made a big rug for the bare cabin floor. After that, the pioneers called Henry's mother The Panther Lady."

"Grandpa, tell us more stories, please."

Grandpa knocked the ashes from his pipe into the fire. "Time for bed, children," he told them.

Tomorrow we get ready for Thanksgiving."

There was much work to do the next day. There were the yams to be washed so their yellow outsides would bake in the hot fireplace ashes. There were pecans to shell to make a cake. The cake would be baked in the Dutch oven on the hearth.

Papa and Grandpa went into the hills and shot a wild turkey gobbler. The children picked the feathers from the turkey. Mama made a cornbread dressing to be baked with pecans and wild river onions while the turkey baked. This would be after the cake was done.

There would be the thick molasses Papa had bought at Fredericksburg. There would be wild honey from the bee trees in the hills. Grandma was churning the yellow butter which she would mold in the butter mold. The butter mold dash had a fern leaf carved on the face of the dash. When it pressed down on the butter it made a pretty fern. The butter looked so pretty.

Then there would be the two fat loaves of wheat bread Mama had baked.

It was going to be such a fine Thanksgiving.

There was sunshine on the hills that Thanksgiving Day. The little birds came out and hopped around the cabin. They were looking for the crumbs Mama and Grandma threw out the kitchen door.

Squirrels ran up and down the tree trunks and leaped from one tree top to another. Tabby brought her three kittens from under the cabin. They had their eyes open now. They tumbled happily over each other in the warm sunshine.

The hills were bright now with the color of autumn. Wild turkey gobblers made the hills ring with their gobbling. Two fawn deer chased each other across the little valleys between the hills.

And then it was noon.

Everybody sat around the table. Grandma brought the big family Bible to the table. Grandpa began to read:

"I will lift up my eyes to the hills, from whence comes my help."

Through the cabin door the children could see the bright hills. It seemed to them the hills heard what Grandpa read. They knew all the secrets Grandpa read about in the Bible.

But the hills
did not
tell.

Words To Remember

quilts	knocked	wheat
comforters	onions	Tabby
handed	molasses	autumn
capered	carved	picked
crook	tumbled	pressed
skinned	fawn	begged

DEER are still plentiful

in the Hill Country.

IV

December came. Grandma and Mama talked soft secrets to each other. The children did not know what they said but they knew the secrets were about Christmas. Some days Grandma sat for hours behind the big curtain around her bed. The children knew Grandma was making presents for Christmas.

Grandpa sat on the south side of the cabin and whittled. He would not let the children come on the south side. Grandpa was whittling presents for Christmas. The children loved it all. It seemed to them that secrets were everywhere, even in the air.

There was wood to be hauled for the fireplace. The children helped. They piled the wood high at the back of the chimney. They would be happy to have the wood when the days and nights grew colder and colder and colder.

In the night the children heard strange sounds. "The trees are groaning," they told each other in the dark of the night.

The next morning they saw what made the strange noise. A heavy snow had fallen in the night. most of the trees had shed their leaves. But liveoak trees do not shed their leaves in the winter. They wait until spring.

Snow had covered the liveoaks with their green leaves. Their limbs were heavy with snow. The limbs broke off from the trunks. "Poor liveoaks," the children said, "they are groaning because their limbs have broken off. The liveoaks are sad."

Papa and Grandpa walked through the snow to feed the animals. The horses had a ridge of snow up and down their backs. The oxen stamped and shook their big horns to get rid of the snow. The cow that gave them milk had a mound of snow between her horns. Her calf had a little white ball of it frozen on the end of its tail.

The chickens were roosting high in the trees. They would not come down for their feed. They were afraid of the snow.

Grandma and Mama were happy to have a well of water at the kitchen door.

The children hurried to eat their good hot mush with thick cow cream poured on top. They buttered Mama's hot biscuits fast. Mama said she made biscuits that morning because it had snowed. The children could not get outside fast enough.

They made a snow man. He had button eyes from Mama's box of buttons. They put Grandpa's old glasses on his nose. They made a black bow tie under his chin. They drew a happy mouth and put buttons up and down his fat stomach. Then they got Papa's old worn out hat for his head. Papa said he needed his hat but he wore his cap so the children could put a hat on their snowman.

They thought the snowman looked so fine.

They named him Clarence. They talked to Clarence. They told him their secrets. And that made Clarence happy.

The hills were covered with a blanket of snow. And where the hills ran down to little valleys the children thought the snow looked like the folds of a big white blanket.

The Hill Country was a lovely land when it was covered with snow.

Water froze in the cedar bucket inside the cabin. The children scooped up fresh snow and poured milk and honey over it. It made ice milk. They loved it. It had such a good taste.

They had venison to eat that day. Venison is deer meat. Papa roasted it over the fire. Then he made some jerky.

He made jerky by cutting the venison into strips. Then he put salt and pepper on the strips. He hung the strips on Mama's clothes line to dry. That is the way pioneers made jerky. After it dried, Mama and Grandma put it in jars. It made good eating while sitting around the fire on cold winter nights.

The snow began to melt and the children were not happy. For every day Clarence melted a little bit more. "Clarence," they begged, "stay with us. We love you." But Clarence's hat slid down his back. His button eyes slid down his fat cheeks. His glasses slid down with his bow tie. Even his happy smile was gone. "Good-bye, Clarence," the children told him. "We will see you next winter."

The next morning Clarence was gone.

That night when the children fed Tabby and her kittens, Grandpa took his pipe out of his mouth and said, "Tabby has two lady cats and one tom cat."

"Grandpa, tell us your secret. How do you know?"

"Well, children, I will let you in on this secret. You see two of these kittens have three colors. See the brown and yellow and black colors. Kittens with three colors are lady kittens. The other cat has just two colors. I think he is a tom cat. Usually kittens with two or one color are."

"More secrets, Grandpa. Tell us more secrets."

"Time for bed, children. Time for bed."

Christmas came. The children wanted snow for Christmas. They wanted to make Clarence come back. But Christmas brought winter winds. The strong winds howled about the cabin. The dogs curled up on some old rugs in the dog run. Papa called the bad winds a blue Texas norther.

Christmas Eve. That night as the family sat around the hearth, Grandpa read again from the Bible:

"And she brought forth her firstborn son and wrapped him in swaddling clothes and laid him in a manger; because there was no room for then in the inn."

Outside, the winds stopped. The night grew still and the stars came out for just a little while. Peace lay all about the cabin. The big clock said, "Tick, tock, tick, tock." The stockings hung from the mantel. Papa banked the coals of fire with ashes. Grandpa put away the Bible. Grandma and Mama slid the warming pans inside woolen bags and put them under the covers at the foot of the beds.

A wolf howled from the hills. Time for bed. Time for Santa Claus to come.

A big fire was blazing in the fireplace the next morning when the children woke. They lay in their warm beds and smelled the good breakfast Grandma and Mama were cooking. They heard Papa grinding the coffee berries in the coffee mill. They could smell the bacon made from the wild hogs in the hills. They smelled fresh eggs. And, oh, Mama was making flapjacks to eat with the good butter and molasses. The pioneers called pan cakes flapjacks. If they were made from cornmeal they were called hoe cakes.

Christmas! The children fell out of their beds.

Each stocking was stuffed with candy. Some had been bought at Fredericksburg. Some was molasses taffy the children had helped pull before Christmas. There were corn shuck dolls for the girls and willow whistles for the boys. There were knitted shawls for Grandma and Mama and knitted gloves for Grandpa and Papa.

The dogs had bones to chew. Tabby and her kittens had red knitted neckties and the cow and her calf each had a red knitted band to tie on their tails. The horses and oxen had extra feedings of corn and the chickens had warm cornmeal mash.

It was such a lovely Christmas.

January was a wild month. It rained and the rain froze in icicles. All the trees had icicles and they hung from the cabin like candy. The tall grasses were iced over and the hills were a fairyland of ice.

The children gathered icicles and made ice cream. Grandma and Mama used thick cream with honey and eggs. They filled the ice cream can, then they put icicles around the can and poured salt over them to make them colder. The children turned the can until the cream got hard. Was it good!

The children wanted so very much for it to snow so they could bring Clarence back. But it would not snow. The winds howled and howled and the little furry creatures went to their dens. They had been eating and eating until they were very fat. Now they could sleep until spring.

Grandpa stepped into a hole that had been iced over and sprained his ankle. Now he had to walk on crutches. His ankle hurt him until he had to stay inside the cabin. Grandpa was not happy. Pioneer men liked to stay outside even when there was rain and wind and snow.

And then it was February. Still no snow, "Oh, why does it not snow," the children wondered. "We want to make Clarence come again."

They dreamed at night that Clarence came. They dreamed that Clarence ran and played with them. But Clarence did not come.

"Clarence will come again next winter," Grandpa told them.

But
    next winter
        was a
            long way
                off.

Words To Remember

curtain	roosting	flapjacks
whittling	cedar	shawls
strange	jerky	icicles
groaning	stomach	sprained
ridge	howled	crutches
stamped	curled	wondered

CLARENCE, the snowman.

BLUEBONNETS cover the hillsides

in the spring.

V

Spring came. The winds grew warm. Green grass peeped above the ground. Leaf buds came out on the tree limbs.

The wildflowers came.

Grandpa read from the big Bible:

"For lo the winter is past,
The rain is over and gone;
The flowers appear on the earth;
The time of the singing of birds
is come...."

Grandpa hobbled on his crutches and told the children the names of the wildflowers growing on the hills and in the valleys. "The Texas Hill Country in the spring is one big blanket of flowers," he said.

Texas bluebonnets covered the hills with a sea of blue. "See their blooms," Grandpa said. "The bloom stems are three to four inches high. The stems are covered with tiny bonnets of blue. Now and then you will find a plant with pink bonnets; sometimes you will find a plant with white bonnets. All other plants, though, have little bonnets of blue."

The children thought the bluebonnets looked exactly like Grandma's and Mama's sunbonnets.

33

Grandpa waved his crutch at a little valley of pink flowers. "That little pink flower covering the ground is the sweet William, sometimes called the wild phlox. If you pull a flower and suck its stem you will find it has a sweet taste."

"Grandpa, see this little vine how it hugs the ground. It smells sweet and has little pink balls. When you smell the little balls they leave yellow dust on your nose."

"That little vine is called the shame vine because it is so bashful if you touch its leaves they curl up and pretend to go to sleep. Sometimes it is called the go-to-sleep vine. And that yellow dust that gets on your nose is pollen. Bees carry pollen dust on their legs to make bee bread for the bees."

"Oh, Grandpa, did you ever see so many wildflowers!"

"The snow did more than give you children Clarence. It made the earth wet way down where the flower seeds sleep. They sleep through the winter. Then the seeds swell and come alive. They open and little stems and leaves come out of the seeds and push their way above the ground. Later on in the spring you will see the daisy families that grow in the Hill Country."

Grandpa rested on his crutches and looked off to where the hills seemed to meet the sky. Then he said:

"The little field daisy bunches close to the ground. Its flowers have white petals around a yellow center. The field daisy is good for cows to eat."

Then Grandpa told them about a daisy with big red petals. It blooms in the summer.

Sometimes it is called firewheel but Grandpa said its real name was Indian Blanket. "The Comanche Indians named it. They had a legend about the Indian Blanket flower. Also, they had another legend about the bluebonnet."

"Grandpa, tell us these legends!"

"Well, if we can sit under that big postoak down by the creek. My ankle hurts."

Grandpa sat down under the big postoak. He leaned his crutch against the tree. Then he told the legend of the Indian blanket:

"Once upon a time a Comanche chief and his braves went to war against some other Indian tribes. While they were away the chief's wife began weaving a warm blanket for the chief when he returned from war. It was a pretty blanket. Its colors were red, yellow and green.

"The chief's little daughter watched her mother weave the colors into the blanket. Then she grew tired and wandered away far into the forest.

"Soon she was lost."

"Night fell. The little Indian girl was cold. She thought of the warm blanket her mother was weaving. She prayed to the Great Spirit to send her a warm blanket with colors of red, yellow and green. Then she lay down and went to sleep.

"The chief and his braves returned in the night. When morning came, he and his braves set out to find the chief's little daughter.

"They found her sleeping under wildflowers whose colors were red, yellow and green.

"These flowers shall be called Indian blankets, the chief told his braves."

"Oh, Grandpa, what a lovely legend. Now

WILD flowers make the

Hill Country beautiful.

tell us the bluebonnet legend."

"You children are in such a big hurry," Grandpa said. Then he took his pipe out of his mouth and began:

"Once upon a time there was a big drought in the Hill Country. A drought is when it does not rain and it does not rain.

"The chief of the Comanche tribe in the Hill Country called his braves to a big pow-wow. A pow-wow is like a big meeting. The chief told his braves he had prayed to the Great Spirit to send rain. The Great Spirit told the chief he could not send rain until someone in the tribe took his dearest possession to the highest hill and offered it to the Great Spirit.

On the edge of the pow-wow sat the chief's little daughter. She held her doll made of corncob and shucks. The little doll wore a bonnet made from the bright feathers of the blue jay bird.

"Her doll was the little girl's dearest possession.

"That night when the Indians were asleep in their teepees, the little girl crept outside. She carried her doll to the highest hill and left it there for the Great Spirit.

"That night it rained, and when morning came, the hill was covered with a flower whose blooms were the shape and color of the little doll's bonnet."

"Oh, Grandpa, what another lovely legend. Now can you tell us some more legends?"

Grandpa smoked his pipe for a while. The children thought he would never begin.

Presently he said, "This story I am going to

tell you is not a legend. Did you know Indians had postoffices?"

"Postoffices, Grandpa what did their postoffices look like? Were they built of stone or wood?"

"Usually their postoffice was a hollow stump. You see, there were times when the braves had to leave their tribes. Sometimes it was to hunt buffalo for meat; sometimes in a drought it was to hunt a land where there was water. If they were gone for a long time, their tribes had to move to a new land. So they left a letter in the postoffice for the braves when they returned.

"They got long slim rocks and laid them side by side in the hollow stump postoffice. If the tribe went west, they pointed the rocks west. If it would take five days for them to get to their new hunting ground, they used five rocks and pointed them west.

"When the braves returned, they read the letter then threw the rocks away. They did not want another tribe reading their letter." Grandpa looked at the children. "Is that not the reason you tear your letters; you do not want someone reading your letter?"

"Grandpa, you know so many, many Hill Country secrets."

Grandpa knew more secrets
   but he
     did not
      tell
The hills knew many, many more secrets
   but they
     did not
      tell.

Words To Remember

voice	weaving	peeped
blanket	returned	hobbled
William	watched	stems
pollen	forest	pink
bunches	meant	families
wheel	postoffices	petals
legend	pointed	leaned
drought	offered	chief
possession	daughter	Great Spirit
edge	real	tee pees
feathers	crept	hollow
crept	shame	laid

DINNER time in

the Hill Country.

VI

Grandpa and Papa cut brush to fence a garden. The children dragged the brush to the little valley where there would be a garden.

Warm rains fell on the land. Yellow buttercups bloomed close to the ground.

The little valley was new soil. The new soil was happy to grow a garden.

There were not enough seeds to plant the garden after the soil was dug up. Grandpa had to make the long trip to Fredericksburg for more seed. It was after Easter before he returned home. Then Grandpa had another story to tell the children.

"Children, this is not a once-upon-a-time story. This story happened while I was at Fredericksburg. It happened on Easter Eve. And it happened to the little children at Fredericksburg and to their mothers.

"The pioneers at Fredericksburg are German. They came from far away Germany across the ocean. They sailed on ships for weeks before they landed at Indianola. They were good pioneers. They wanted to come to the Texas Hill Country because it was a new land.

"They wanted to begin a new life in a new land.

"There were Indians in the hills around Fredericksburg. Some of these Indians were on the warpath.

"The pioneers at Fredericksburg wanted peace with the Indians. Meusebach, the man who founded Fredericksburg, was going to meet with the great Comanche chiefs at the San Saba River. The men at Fredericksburg went with Meusebach. They left many weeks before Easter to meet with these great Indian chiefs. The San Saba River was many miles away from Fredericksburg. There were no roads. They had to travel through a wilderness.

"Easter Eve came. The men had not returned. They should have been home by now. The good German wives were worried. But they began baking pies and cakes and yeast breads. Soon every cabin was filled with the good smells of Easter foods.

"Night fell. The men had not returned.

"A little German girl looked at the hills. She saw bright fires blazing in the hills. She was afraid. 'Mother, what are those fires in the hills? I can count them; I can see one, two, three, four, five fires..What are they, Mother?'

"The poor mother was afraid. She wondered why the Indians burned these fires in the hills. But she must not let the little girl know it was Indians.

" 'It is the Easter Rabbit, Little one.' the mother said. 'It is the Easter Rabbit dyeing his eggs. He picks the bright-colored wildflowers and boils them in his big pots to make the dyes for his Easter eggs.'

"Now the little girl was happy. She told the

good news to all the other children in Fredericksburg. They thought of all the lovely dyes the Easter Rabbit could make from the many colors of the wildflowers.

"All night that Easter Eve the fires burned in the hills. And all night the mothers watched and prayed.

"Early the next morning they heard the happy sound of the church bells ringing. The bells were telling the mothers and the children not to be afraid to come to church. The Easter fires burning in the hills were peace fires. The men had returned. They had made
    peace
      with
        the
          Indians.''

Words To Remember

Easter	dragged	soil
warpath	happened	German
founded	peace	Meusebach
blazing	wilderness	yeast
spread	dyeing	boils

Meusebach—Moys-e-baa

VII

But some Indians still were on the warpath. The United States Government built forts all up and down the west side of the Hill Country. These forts were built some fifty miles apart.

Soldiers lived in these forts. They lived in the forts so they could protect the pioneers from the Indians. As long as the soldiers were at the forts, the Indians did not make much war on the pioneers.

Then a great war broke out between the people in the north and the people in the south of the United States. The war was over slavery. The Texas Hill Country was in the South. The states in the South had set up their own government. They now called themselves a confederacy. The soldiers became confederate soldiers. This war between the North and the South was called a Civil War.

Now the soldiers had to leave the forts to fight for the Confederate Army. And when the soldiers left the forts, the Indians went on the warpath again. Herman Lehmann was captured in the Hill Country. Fourteen-year-old Alice Todd was captured by the Indians. So was Adolph Korn. Horses were stolen for the Indians loved horses. Women and children were captured. Old men were killed. It was a terrible time for the pioneers in the Texas Hill Country.

The Confederate soldiers had many great leaders but the leader they loved the best was General Robert E. Lee.

On Christmas before the Civil War broke out, General Lee was commander at Fort Mason in the Hill Country. The soldiers wanted to give a Christmas ball and invite the Mason Pioneers. They had no place for the ball so they held it in Commander Lee's headquarters at the fort.

Mrs. Wilson Hey was a young girl living in the little settlement at Mason. She attended the ball. She said Commander Lee did not dance. He enjoyed seeing the others dance but Commander Robert E. Lee was very sad that night. He knew the Civil War was coming and he knew what it would do to the Texas Hill Country when it came.

The war lasted four years. All men able to bear arms had to go to fight. Papa had to go but Grandpa was too old. He stayed at home to help Grandma and Mama.

They tried to have a garden. But in those four years of the war the Longhorn cattle ran wild. These Texas hills were full of wild cows with their long, curved horns.

There were no young men at home during the war to drive them to market so they roamed the Hill Country by the thousands. They ate the gardens; they ate the corn and peas. It was hard for pioneers to keep from starving.

When the war was over and the soldiers came back to their families in the Hill Country,

THE pioneer cattle drives must

have looked something like this.

they found them hungry. They had to find some way to keep their families from starving.

They saw the thousands of Longhorn cattle roaming the hills. They said why not round up these wild cows and trail them to market. The Government had put most of the Indians by that time on reservations. They needed meat to feed these Indians. The soldiers were again at the forts. They had to have meat.

After the war, all of the United States needed meat.

Now began the greatest cattle drives of the Hill Country ever known. And now began the history of the Hill Country cowboys. And they were the greatest cowboys the nation had ever known.

The man at the head of a cow drive was called a drover. He usually trailed some 2,000 head of Longhorns. Sometimes a trail drive was made up of 3,000 head of Longhorns.

It took real cowboys to round up these wild cows in the Texas hills. The cattle would be driven to what was called holding grounds. They were herded there by more cowboys until the cattle were gathered. Then the drive began.

They trailed these Longhorns all the way across Texas. They swam them across the Red River. Now they were in Indian Territory. The Indian Territory later became the state of Oklahoma.

Usually when the drover and his cowboys reached the Indian Territory with their Longhorns, an Indian chief would be waiting with his skinners to ask for beef. The drover knew he must give them beef. If he did not, the Indians would come in the night and stampede the herd.

A stampede is when something scares the cattle and they would begin to run. Usually the cattle stampeded in the night. The cattle would be lying down asleep. A clap of thunder would come out of the sky. Then every cow would jump up at the same time and start running. They would run over anything. Many a cowboy was killed when he tried to turn the wild herd. Sometimes the cattle would run for miles.

After crossing Indian Territory, the drover, his cowboys and his Longhorns would be in Kansas.

One of the most famous towns for receiving the cattle was Dodge City, Kansas.

A cattle drive usually lasted three months.

When Papa came back from one of the cattle drives, he had a funny story to tell the children, about a drive he was on:

A herd of Longhorns was to be trailed through Fredericksburg. There were 2,000 cattle in the herd. They were to be trailed to Kansas. This would be the first Longhorn drive to come through Fredericksburg.

The people of Fredericksburg were happy. Most of them had never seen a trail drive.

Just before the Longhorns reached Fredericksburg, the Concord stage came through. It was on its way to San Antonio. The stage driver heard the cattle were coming. He stopped the stage to see the Longhorns come down Fredericksburg's main street.

Two fancy dressed men on their way to New York got off the stage to see the cattle come

48

through. They had never seen many cows and they had never seen a cowboy.

The Longhorns were nervous as they started up Main Street. All 2,000 had just entered Main Street. The New Yorkers stood on the sidewalk. The Texas sun beat down on them that noon. One of the men opened his bright red umbrella.

That did it.

Those Longhorns went wild. They tore through stores carrying chairs and rugs and plows on their big, curving horns. They tore through cabins and gardens in their wild haste to get out of town.

The cowboys spent the rest of the day rounding up the herd. They were tired. They wished those two fancy dressed New Yorkers had stayed in New York where they belonged.

There was always a cook on those cow drives. He used a chuck box fitted on the end of his wagon. When the chuck box lid was down, it made a good table where the cook could prepare the food for cooking. Usually the food was dry beans, coffee, potatoes, onions and bacon. The cowboys called the bacon side meat because it was sliced off the sides of the hogs. Now and then a beef would be killed for meat. And sometimes, if the cook was in a good humor with the cowboys, he made a cobbler pie with dried peaches or apricots.

Papa told of a stampede one night. "We could not find the cook when the stampede was over," Papa said. "We just knew he had been run over and killed by those wild cows. When daylight came, we found the cook up in the very top of a tall pecan tree. He was afraid to come down. We did not get any breakfast until one of the cowboys went up the tree and talked him into coming down!''

Rich cattle buyers from the East now began coming to the Hill Country ranches. They brought some fifteen or twenty cowboys, a chuck wagon and a *remuda* of horses. To the Hill Country, *remuda* was a Spanish word meaning many horses.

There were no banks in the Hill Country then except where there were a few cities. Cattle buyers brought their money in bags of gold coin to pay for the cattle they bought.

Papa told the children of one buyer from the East who tied his bags of gold around his saddle horn while he rode the ranches, cutting out the cows he wanted to buy.

When he had finished buying his cattle, he could not find the tree where he had hung his money bags.

His cattle had to be held on the holding grounds until he and his cowboys and the ranchers found his money.

This time, it was the trees and not the hills who held
their
secrets.

Words To Remember

United States	Government	protect
Confederate	Civil	Lehmann
captured	General	commander
headquarters	Hey(Hay)	attended
enjoyed	bear	curved
roamed	trail	reservations
nation	drover	gathered
Territory	Oklahoma	stampede
Kansas	receiving	Dodge City
nervous	haste	fancy
dudes	fitted	carrying
prepare	*remuda*	buyers

A Hill Country cowboy.

VIII

The first ranches were fenced with rock. Pioneers knew how to lay the rocks so the fence would not fall down. Sometimes it took as many as three years to fence a ranch with rock.

Then wire was brought to the Hill Country. It did not take so long to build a wire fence.

Some pioneer farmers did not like to see the big ranches fenced off. The fenced ranches shut off roads, water holes, even river crossings. The farmers grew angry. They began cutting the wire fences. This started the wire fence war. Finally the United States Government passed a law making cutting wire fences a penitentiary offense.

There still were wild animals to kill cattle, calves, horses and colts. There was the timber wolf and the panther. There were bob cats and coyotes. And there was the mountain lion.

But the animal the pioneers feared most for their livestock was the lobo wolf. No horse could outrun the lobo wolf. Then the Government put a bounty on wolves. A bounty is when pioneers were paid to kill harmful animals.

Up to now most schools and church services were held in homes. Then the pioneers cut logs and built one-room schools. On Sundays, these one-room schoolhouses were used for church services.

It was hard to get teachers. There was not much money to pay their salaries. The teachers would stay a week with one family. The next week they would stay with another family, and so on until the school term was over. A school term usually lasted three or four months.

There were no desks. The pupils sat on benches. The seats were made of split logs. The logs were made smooth to sit on.

There were few books. Teachers taught the Three R's—reading, writing and arithmetic. The pupils recited poems. They had school plays. They sang songs at school and at church.

Pioneers and most of their children loved the school days and the church services.

Summer came again to the Texas Hill Country. The agarita bushes were red with berries. Pioneers called the agarita algerita.

It was time for the families to go berry hunting. They wanted the juice of the agarita berry to make wines and jellies.

Families gathered to drive in their wagons to the berry flats. They put blankets under the agarita bushes and threshed the berries with sticks.

When the noon sun stood high in the sky they spread their food on a blanket, like a picnic, under a shady liveoak. After all the berry threshing, everything tasted good.

Back home, the women had the children pick out the leaves and little sticks from the berries. Then they cooked the juices. They had little sugar but when sweetened with honey, the juice made a good tasting jelly.

The children ran and played in the hot Texas sun. They learned the secrets of wild animals. They found little nests lined with rabbit fur in the ground. And after a few days, when their eyes were opened, the baby rabbits came out into the world.

The children found the nests of the wild turkey hens. "Never put your hands in a wild creature's nest," Grandpa had always told them. "And don't pet a baby fawn still wearing its spots. When the mothers come back to their young, they will not take them, for they can smell your hands."

Sometimes the children would find a turkey hen feeding on grass seeds or tender plants. The children would hide so they could follow the turkey hen to her nest. But she never went to her nest. Grandpa said she was just leading the children on a "wild goose chase."

They saw the Mama dove drag her leg on the ground and they followed her. Soon they learned her secret. She was not crippled; she was leading the children away from her babies.

Oh, there were so many, many secrets to be learned
   in the
      Texas
         Hill Country.

Words To Remember

angry	coyotes	chase
bounty	services	salaries
board	desks	benches
smooth	recited	poems
agarita	algerita	juice
threshed	spread	picnic

ROCK fences are still in use.

"GENTLE winds still blow

across the hills . . ."

IX

Now you have learned the history of the pioneers in the Texas Hill Country. Perhaps some of you live or have lived in this lovely land.

Austin, the capital of Texas, is located in the Hill Country. Lyndon Baines Johnson, our 36th president, lived in the Hill Country. Perhaps you have visited his home on the Pedernales River.

Fred Gipson, who wrote *Old Yeller*, was born and lived out his life in the Texas Hill Country. You can find his home on the Llano River.

The Mormon people once had a little town and a grist mill in the Hill Country. Their town, in Burnet County, was named Zodiac. Kingsland, Marble Falls and other towns around the Lake Area are tourist resorts today. Buchanan Lake is a tourist attraction.

The little town of Bandera in the Texas Hill Country is known as a cowboy capital because so many rodeo performers live or have lived there. There are dude ranches in that area of the Hill Country where visitors can ride horses on their tours. There are pilgrimages today in the Hill Country. Here, tourists can visit Johnson City named for President Johnson's family. On these tours you can visit President Johnson's home, the

LBJ Park and Ranch. Also, you can visit Luckenbach and Fredericksburg.

You have already read much about Fredericksburg. Did you know that each Easter the people of Fredericksburg still burn the Easter fires in the hills, just as the Comanche Indians burned them on that Easter Eve more than a hundred years ago?

And have you read of the Sunday houses in Fredericksburg? Long ago, pioneers had to drive so far to attend church at Fredericksburg on Sundays they could not drive back home that same day. So they built little houses in Fredericksburg where they could spend the night and drive back to their homes the next day. They called these little houses Sunday houses. Some of these little Sunday houses still stand in Fredericksburg today.

Many of the rock fences built in the Hill Country still stand today.

Have you seen any of the wood carvings done by Gene Zesch who lives in the Texas Hill Country? His carvings tell the story of those days of the Hill Country cowpoke. You will laugh at his carvings but you will love them. They tell a true story of those days long gone by. You can find his carvings in the LBJ Library at Austin.

During the last of March and the first of April each year the Hill Country sponsors the famous Bluebonnet Trail. Tourists from all over the United States take this tour to see the colorful roadside flowers of Indian paintbrush, yellow coreopsis, Indian blankets, daisies and most of all the Texas bluebonnets for which the Hill Country is famous.

Today the Hill Country has paved roads,

electricity, railroads, airports and TV's. And would you believe it, the Longhorn breed of cattle those Texas cowboys once trailed to Kansas and other parts of the United States are coming back to mix with the Hereford, the Black Angus, as well as other fine breeds of cattle?

Herman Lehmann lived nine years with the Indians. When he came back to his Hill Country, he was more Indian in his ways than white.

Alice Todd was never heard of again. Her mother and the black slave girl are buried at the foot of Todd Mountain in the Texas Hill Country.

The big buffalo wallows are filling up. These trails made by the buffalo in the Hill Country became cattle trails for the great Longhorn drives. Now they are covered with grass.

Over a hundred years have gone by. The pioneers learned to love this Texas Hill Country. They handed down this love to their children and to their children's children.

At times there are droughts in the Hill Country and the people make no crops. Times then can grow hard. Other times the Hill Country is a good land of green pastures and ranches and farms. It is a land where families have worked hard and are proud of their homes and of their friendship with each other.

Long ago, when the pioneers first came, the hills looked down on these people and were proud of a people who came on ships, in ox wagons or on horseback. Today those same hills look down with pride at the changes those first people's descendants have made in this land of sloping hills.

Gentle winds still blow across these hills. Sometimes strong, tearing winds blow across them. Snow still blankets the hills, the same as when Clarence came to be with the children. Grasses and wildflowers cover these hills in the spring.

Grandpa has long been gone but he still lives on in the minds and lives of his great, great grand-children, in the colorful wildflowers and in those
    gentle
       rolling
          Texas
         hills.

Words To Remember

visited	Pedernales	Mormons
Zodiac	tourist	resorts
Bandera	pilgrimages	Luckenbach
tour	carvings	Zesch (Zesh)
sponsors	laugh	library
famous	paved	coreopsis
Hereford	Angus	electricity
wallows	friendship	buried